Diabetic M Prep For Beginners 2021

Essential Diet Guide to Cure Diabetes by Eating Nutritionally-Balanced Meal to Live Healthy with Delicious Recipes and a 7-Day Meal Plan

BOB KERRY

Table of Contents

DISCLAIMER

Please note that the information in this book are written for the express purpose of sharing educational information only. The information herein is stated to be reliable and consistence but the author neither implies nor intends any guarantee of accuracy for specific cases or individuals.

It is recommended that you consult a licensed professional before beginning any practice relating to your health, diet, or lifestyle. The contents of this book are not replacement for professional advice.

The author, publisher and distributors disclaim any liability, loss or damage and risk taken by individuals who directly or indirectly act on the information contained in this book.

INTRODUCTION

Diabetes Mellitus popularly known as simply "Diabetes" is a serious disease that occurs when your body has difficulty properly regulating the amount of dissolved sugar (glucose) in your blood stream. It is unrelated to a similarly named disorder "Diabetes Insipidus" which involves kidney-related fluid retention problems.

In order to understand diabetes, it is necessary to first understand the role glucose plays with regard to the body, and what can happen when regulation of glucose fails and blood sugar levels become dangerously low or high.

The tissues and cells that make up the human body are living things, and require food to stay alive. The food cells eat is a type of sugar called glucose. Fixed in place as they are, the body's cells are completely dependent on the blood stream in which they are bathed to bring glucose to them. Without access to adequate glucose, the body's cells have nothing to fuel themselves with and soon die.

Our bodies function best at a certain level of sugar in the bloodstream. If the amount of sugar in our blood runs too high or too low, then we typically feel bad. Diabetes is the most common endocrine disorder. It was estimated that sixteen million Americans have diabetes, yet many are not aware of it. African-Americans, Hispanics, and Native Americans have a higher rate of developing diabetes during their lifetime. Diabetes has potential long term complications that can affect the kidneys, eyes, heart, blood vessels, and nerves.

What is glucose?

Glucose is a simple sugar found in food. Glucose is an essential nutrient that provides energy for the proper functioning of the body cells. Carbohydrates are broken down in the small intestine and the glucose in digested food is then absorbed by the intestinal cells into the bloodstream, and is carried by the bloodstream to all the cells in the body where it is utilized. However, glucose cannot enter the cells alone and needs insulin to aid in its transport into the cells. Without insulin, the cells become starved of glucose energy despite the presence of abundant glucose in the bloodstream. In certain types of diabetes, the cells' inability to utilize glucose gives rise to the ironic situation of "starvation in the midst of plenty". The abundant, unutilized glucose is wastefully excreted in the urine.

What is insulin?

Insulin is a hormone that is produced by specialized cells (beta cells) of the pancreas. (The pancreas is a deep-seated organ in the abdomen located behind the stomach.) In addition to helping glucose enter the cells, insulin is also important in tightly regulating the level of glucose in the blood. After a meal, the blood glucose level rises. In response to the increased glucose level, the pancreas normally releases more insulin into the bloodstream to help glucose enter the cells and lower blood glucose levels after a meal. When the blood glucose levels are lowered, the insulin release from the pancreas is turned down. It is important to note that even in the fasting state there is a low steady release of insulin than fluctuates a bit and helps to maintain a steady blood sugar level during fasting. In normal individuals, such a regulatory system helps to keep blood glucose levels in a tightly controlled range. As stated above, in patients with diabetes, the insulin is either absent, relatively insufficient for the body's needs, or not used properly by the body. All of these factors cause elevated levels of blood glucose (hyperglycemia).

Types of Diabetes

Although doctors and patients alike tend to group all patients with diabetes together, the truth is that there are two different types of diabetes which are similar in their elevated blood sugar, but different in many other ways. Throughout the remainder of these web pages we will be referring to the different types of diabetes when appropriate, but when the topic pertains to both types of diabetes we will use the general term "diabetes".

Diabetes is correctly divided into two major subgroups:

- Type 1 diabetes
- Type 2 diabetes

This division is based upon whether the blood sugar problem is caused by insulin deficiency (type 1) or insulin resistance (type 2). Insulin deficiency means there is not enough insulin being made by the pancreas due to a malfunction of their insulin producing cells. Insulin resistance occurs when there is plenty of insulin made by the pancreas (it is functioning normally and making plenty of insulin), but the cells of the body are resistant to its action which results in the blood sugar being too high.

Type 1 diabetes is an autoimmune disease that impacts 1.25 million American children and adults. The immune system destroys the cells that release insulin, eventually leading to the complete inability to produce insulin in the body. Type 1 generally manifests at a young age and lasts a lifetime.

Type 2 diabetes has multiple contributing factors including genetics and lifestyle factors such as obesity and inactivity. The disease generally arises during adulthood and oftentimes can be reversed or controlled through diet and exercise. 90-95% of those diagnosed with diabetes have type 2.

There are other types of diabetes apart from the major ones:

Prediabetes which happens when the blood sugar is above the normal level, but it's not high enough for a diagnosis of type 2 diabetes.

Gestational diabetes is high blood sugar during pregnancy. It is caused by Insulin-blocking hormones produced by the placenta.

Note: Diabetes insipidus should not be mistaken to be one of the diabetes (Diabetes Mellitus) in discussion here. As mentioned earlier, It's a different rare condition which involves kidney-related fluid retention problems.

Signs and Symptoms of Diabetes

Type 1 and type 2 diabetes share similar symptoms. However, those with type 2 diabetes may not experience signs before a diagnosis because symptoms may surface gradually. Those diagnosed with Type 1 diabetes generally seek medical attention when symptoms become noticeable.

General Diabetes Symptoms

- Dry, itchy skin (skin problems)
- Hunger
- Fatigue and tiredness
- Blurred vision
- Frequent urination
- Weight loss
- Slow-healing wounds
- Excessive thirst
- Tingling sensation in feet
- Yeast infections

Men Diabetes Symptoms

- Erectile dysfunction (impotence)
- Lower testosterone levels

- Retrograde ejaculation
- Decreased sex drive

Women Diabetes Symptoms

- Polycystic ovary syndrome
- Vaginal itching and soreness
- Oral thrush
- Urinary Tract Infection (UTI)

Diabetes and Diet

For Type 1 Diabetes

Type 1 Diabetes is an autoimmune problem that leads to the body's inability to produce insulin and last a life time (meaning a patient will need treatment for the rest of their lives) which mostly occur at a very young age.

Type 1 diabetes is rare and it can be managed by eating healthy along with other medical treatment. There is nothing like a distinct diet pattern for type 1 diabetics. A healthy diet means having a balance of protein, carbohydrates and fat. It's important to include plenty of vegetables and fruit. A healthy diet is recommended for everyone. However, the most important thing for type-1 diabetics to consider is whether foods have carbohydrates in or not. It's also important to be aware how quickly the carbohydrates are absorbed by the body. Understanding these things make it easier to know when and how much insulin to inject to cover the carbohydrate in whatever you are eating.

Foods like bread, pasta, and rice are high in carbohydrates, but it's also important to remember that many fruits also contain a lot of carbs. If you are eating a meal with a lot of carbohydrate, you will need to inject more insulin to cover it. If you are eating something with little or no carbohydrate, you may need to avoid taking any quick-acting insulin at all. Once an insulin regime is established it is possible to include such things as chocolate or a dessert so long as it is possible to work out the extra insulin that's needed to cover them.

For Type 2 Diabetes

Type 2 diabetes is the most common diabetes affecting 90-95 percent of the diabetic patients. It can be cure if given proper attention through diet and some other lifestyle changes.

A diagnosis of type 2 diabetes or even prediabetes usually means the doctor has suggested that you make some changes to your diet to help relieve your symptoms and regulate your blood sugar. This is a good time to become wiser about how you are eating on a regular basis.

Fortunately, following a diabetes diet doesn't mean giving up the joy of eating or avoiding your favorite foods and special family meals. You can still enjoy "pizza night," celebrate anniversaries, and partake in holiday meals and vacation dining.

This is more about your routine daily food choices and meal planning.

Eating to beat diabetes is much more about making wise food adjustments than it is about denial and deprivation. A better way to look at a diet when you have diabetes is one that helps you establish a new normal when it comes to your eating habits and food choices.

Following a Healthy Diabetic-Focused Diet

For those with prediabetes or type 2 diabetes, the main focus of a diabetes-focused diet is being attentive to your weight. Keeping weight in check, being active, and picking the right foods to eat can help prevent most cases of type 2 diabetes.

To follow a healthy diet for diabetes, you must first understand how different foods affect your blood sugar.

Carbohydrates, which are found to the largest degree in grains, bread, pasta, milk, sweets, fruit, and starchy vegetables, are broken down into glucose in the blood, which raises blood sugar, potentially leading to hyperglycemia.

Protein and fats have little, if any, impact on blood sugar. However, both should be consumed in moderation along with carbs to keep calories down and weight in a healthy range.

To hit your blood sugar level target, eat a variety of foods but monitor portions for foods with a high carbohydrate content. Foods high in carbohydrates have the most impact on blood sugar level. This is why some people with diabetes count their carbohydrates at meals and snacks.

Foods Encouraged to Eat By Type 2 Diabetics

PROTEINS

- Fish high in omega-3 fatty acids, such as salmon, sardines, Albacore tuna, mackerel, and rainbow trout
- Shellfish, including clams, crab, imitation shellfish, lobster, scallops, shrimps, and oysters
- Skinless turkey
- Skinless chicken
- Beans and legumes
- Cottage cheese
- Nuts and nut spreads, like almond butter (in moderation)
- Whole eggs
- Tofu

GRAINS

- Wild or brown rice
- Quinoa
- Barley

- Whole-grain breads, such as 100 percent whole-wheat bread (check that each slice offers at least 3 g of fiber)
- Whole-grain cereal, such as steel-cut oats
- Whole-wheat pasta

DIARY

- Unsweetened almond milk
- Unsweetened soy milk
- Nonfat plain Greek yogurt
- Nonfat, low-sodium cottage cheese
- Reduced-fat cheese (in moderation)
- Nonfat, unsweetened kefir
- Skim milk

VEGETABLES

- Greens, like spinach, kale, and Swiss chard
- Cruciferous veggies, like broccoli and cauliflower
- Cucumbers
- Asparagus
- Jicama

- Brussels sprouts
- Onions
- Artichoke hearts
- Peppers
- Beets

(Eat the Following in Moderation)

- Corn
- White potatoes
- Sweet potatoes
- Yams
- Peas

FRUITS

- Berries, like blueberries, strawberries, and raspberries
- Apples with the skin on
- Peaches with the skin on
- Tart cherries
- Apricots with the skin on
- Pears with the skin on
- Oranges

- Kiwi

- Bananas

- Grapes

- Melon

FATS (GOOD SOURCES OF FATS)

- Avocados

- Nuts, like almonds, cashews, pecans, walnuts, and peanuts

- Nut butters

- Olives

- Plant-based oils, like soybean oil, corn oil, olive oil, and sunflower oil

- Seeds, like flaxseed and chia seed

- Fish, like salmon and tuna

- Tofu

Foods Discouraged to Eat By Type 2 Diabetics

PROTEINS

- Many deli meats, like bologna, salami, ham, and roast beef (turkey is an acceptable option)
- Hot dogs
- Sausages and pepperoni
- Beef jerky
- Bacon
- Sweetened or flavored nuts, like honey-roasted or spicy
- Sweetened protein shakes or smoothies

GRAINS

- White bread
- Pastries
- Sugary breakfast cereals

- White rice

- White pasta

FRUITS

- Dried fruit
- Packaged juices
- Canned fruit in syrup

FATS (BAD SOURCES OF FATS)

- Fast food
- Beef, hot dogs, sausage, bacon, spareribs, and salt pork
- Full-fat dairy products
- Coconut and palm oil
- Packaged snacks, like crackers, corn chips, and potato chips
- Processed sweets, like doughnuts, cakes, cookies, and muffins
- Stick margarine and butter

Tips for Diabetics on Eating Healthy

- Eat three meals each day, including breakfast.

- Try not to skip meals.

- Space meals 4 to 6 hours apart.

- Breakfast, lunch and supper should be about the same size.

- Avoid very large or very small meals.

- Have one piece of fresh fruit at each meal.

- Limit juice to 1/2 cup per day.

- Limit your intake to high fat foods, including deep fried or fried foods.

- Limit meat portions to the size of the palm of your hand and choose

- Fish or skinless poultry more often.

- Be careful of added fats. Choose low fat or fat free dressings or spreads.

Sample 7-Day Diabetic Meal Plan

Here's a sample seven-day meal plan to portray the idea of how easy it really is to eat healthy without depriving yourself when you have type 2 diabetes.

DAY 1

Breakfast

- 1 cup oatmeal
- 1 tbsp sliced almonds
- 1 tbsp ground flaxseed

Total carb: 30 grams

Lunch

- Turkey sandwich on
- 2 slices whole wheat bread
- Raw veggies
- Hummus dip Total carbohydrate: ~45 grams carbohydrate

Total carb: 30 - 40 grams

Dinner

- 3 oz grilled salmon
- ½ cup baked potato
- Spinach salad
- 1 cup skim milk

Total carb: 30 - 40 grams

DAY 2

Breakfast

- Scrambled egg beaters on
- whole wheat english muffin

Total carb: 30 grams

Lunch

- 1 cup bean soup
- Green salad

Total carb: 30 - 40 grams

Dinner

- Chicken or steak stir-fry with plenty of vegetables
- ⅔ cup brown rice

Total carb: 30 - 40 grams

DAY 3

Breakfast

- 1 cup oatmeal
- 1 tbsp sliced almonds
- 1 tbsp ground flaxseed

Total carb: 30 grams

Lunch

- ½ cup tuna fish salad on
- 1 whole tomato
- 6 oz light yogurt
- 1 fruit

Total carb: 30 - 40 grams

Dinner

- 3 oz grilled chicken breast
- 1 cup baked acorn squash
- 1 cup steamed broccoli
- 1 cup skim milk

Total carb: 30 - 40 grams

DAY 4

Breakfast

- ¾ cup whole grain cereal (or Glucerna cereal)
- 1 cup skim milk

Total carb: 30 grams

Lunch

- 1 cup vegetable soup
- ½ turkey sandwich on
- 1 whole wheat bread
- Raw veggies

Total carb: 30 - 40 grams

Dinner

- Spaghetti dinner
- 1 cup spaghetti squash
- ½ cup spaghetti sauce
- Tossed green salad

Total carb: 30 - 40 grams

DAY 5

Breakfast

- 1 cup oatmeal
- 1 tbsp sliced almonds
- 1 tbsp ground flaxseed

Total carb: 30 grams

Lunch

- Low-fat cottage cheese on
- 1 whole tomato
- 4 Ak-Mak crackers

- 1 fruit

Total carb: 30 - 40 grams

<u>Dinner</u>

- 2 slices thin crust veg pizza
- Romaine lettuce salad

Total carb: 30 - 40 grams

DAY 6

<u>Breakfast</u>

- 2 slices french toast made from whole wheat bread
- Sugar-free maple syrup

Total carb: 30 grams

<u>Lunch</u>

- Large green salad with grilled chicken breast
- 1 cup skim milk
- 1 fruit

Total carb: 30 - 40 grams

Dinner

- 3 oz pan-seared trout
- 1 cup stir-fried vegetables
- ⅔ cup brown rice

Total carb: 30 - 40 grams

DAY 7

Breakfast

- Scrambled Egg Beaters omelet with vegetables
- 2 slices whole wheat toast
- Sliced tomatoes

Total carb: 30 grams

Lunch

- Turkey sandwich on
- 2 slices whole wheat bread
- Raw veggies

- Hummus dip

Total carb: 30 - 40 grams

Dinner

- Chicken and bean burrito with
- Whole wheat low-carb tortilla
- Salsa or pico de gallo
- Green salad

Total carb: 30 - 40 grams

SAMPLE SNACKS TO EAT

If Your Blood Sugar is Over 140 (NO CARB SNACKS)

- Raw veggies and dip
- Tomato with low-fat cottage cheese
- 2-4 tbsp almonds
- Tomato with tuna salad
- Celery sticks with peanut butter
- Tomato with fresh low-fat mozarella

- Cheese, balsamic and olive oil
- Hard cooked egg

If Your Blood Sugar is 100 -140 (15g CARB SNACKS)

- 1 cup strawberries
- 1 carton light yogurt with
- 2 tbsp ground flax seed
- 1 medium orange
- ½ banana
- ½ cup applesauce
- 3 cups light popcorn
- ½ cup light ice cream

If Your Blood Sugar is Less Than 100 (30g CARB SNACKS)

- 2 cups mixed berries and melon
- 1 carton light yogurt and

- 1 cup strawberries
- 1 orange and
- ¾ ounce pretzels
- 1 whole banana
- ½ cup applesauce and
- 3 squares graham cracker
- 6 cups light popcorn
- 1 cup light ice cream

The General Guideline of the Meal Plan

Below is what we want to achieve with the meal plan. There are choice of snacks to take with dinner, lunch or breakfast. The specification is there for you to choose.

For instance if someone wants to take 60g per meal; after following the breakfast meal here which gives 30g, snacks that can give 30g will be choosen alongside to achieve the aim. The guidelines is as follows:

- Carbohydrates Women: 30-45 grams per meal
- Men: 45-60 grams per meal
- Fiber 25-35 grams per day
- Fat 1200 cal: 33 grams fat, 9 grams saturated fat
- 1500 cal: 42 grams fat, 12 grams saturated fat
- 1800 cal: 50 grams fat, 14 grams saturated fat
- Sodium 1,500 mg per day (500 mg per meal)

RECIPES

Beef with Noodles

Prep Time: 10 minutes

Cook Time: 10 minutes

Total Time: 20 minutes

Servings: 1

Ingredients

- 1 (3-ounce) package ramen noodles, seasoning packet discarded
- 1 pound 90% lean ground beef
- 1 green bell pepper, chopped
- 1/2 cup onion, chopped
- 1 can (14.5-ounce) diced tomatoes with roasted garlic
- 1 teaspoon Italian seasoning
- 1 teaspoon garlic powder

- 1/4 teaspoon salt
- 1/4 teaspoon black pepper

Instructions

1. Cook noodles according to package directions; rinse and drain.

2. In a medium nonstick skillet over medium-high heat, brown ground beef. Remove beef and drain.

3. In same skillet, over medium heat, cook bell pepper and onions 5 to 6 minutes or until tender, stirring occasionally. Add tomatoes, beef, Italian seasoning, garlic powder, salt, and pepper. Cook 5 to 7 minutes, or until heated through, stirring occasionally.

4. Stir in noodles, and cook for 1 to 2 minutes. Serve.

Note

Choosing extra-lean ground beef is always a smart option when following a diabetic diet, because it eliminates some extra fat and calories. We've got more meaty, easy dinner recipes in our collection of diabetic-friendly ground beef recipes.

Chargrilled Vegetable Salad

Prep Time: 20 minutes

Cook Time: 1 hour

Total Time: 1 hour 20 minutes

Servings: 6

Ingredients

- 2 red peppers
- 3 tablespoons olive oil
- 1 tablespoon red wine vinegar
- 1 small garlic clove , crushed
- 1 red chilli , deseeded, finely chopped
- 1 aubergine , cut into 1cm rounds
- 2 red onions , sliced about 1.5cm thick but kept as whole slices

- 6 plump sundried tomatoes in oil, drained and torn into strips
- handful black olives
- large handful basil , roughly torn

Instructions

1. First, blacken the peppers all over (do this directly over a flame, over hot coals or under a hot grill). When completely blackened, put them in a bowl, cover with a plate and leave to cool.

2. While the peppers are cooling, mix the oil, vinegar, garlic and chilli in a large bowl. On a hot barbecue or griddle pan, chargrill the aubergine, courgette and onions in batches until they have defined grill marks on both sides and are starting to soften. The time will depend on the intensity of your grill, so use your judgement – courgettes and red onions are fine still slightly crunchy but you want the aubergine cooked all the way through. As the

vegetables are ready, put them straight into the dressing to marinate, breaking the onions up into rings.

3. When the peppers are cool enough to handle, peel, remove the stalk and scrape out the seeds. Cut into strips and toss through the veg with any juice from the bowl. Mix in the tomatoes, olives, basil and seasoning. Drizzle with more oil, if you like, and serve either on its own or with mozzarella or crumbled feta.

Gluten Free Avocado Bread

Prep Time: 20 minutes

Cook Time: 15 minutes

Total Time: 35 minutes

Servings: 4

Ingredients

- 1 cup coconut flour

- 4 tablespoons psyllium husks
- 4 tablespoons nutritional yeast
- 4 tablespoons coconut oil, melted (use olive oil if you prefer)
- 1/2 teaspoon truffle salt, (use sea salt if you prefer)
- ¼ teaspoon ground black pepper
- 2 cups just-boiled water
- 1 ripe, Fresh California Avocado, divided (mash 1/2 to go into the flatbread, and slice the remaining 1/2 for topping)
- 1 tablespoon avocado cooking oil
- 1/4 teaspoon sea salt, or to taste
- 1 large heirloom tomato, sliced
- 1 1/2 cups microgreens or baby arugula

Instructions

1. Mix coconut flour, husks, and nutritional yeast in a medium bowl. Mix in the coconut or olive oil and the seasoning.

2. Add the just-boiled water (best is JUST off the boil) and combine well with a wooden spoon.

3. As soon as the dough becomes tolerable to handle (not too hot), gently fold in mashed avocado. Use your hands to gently form it into a ball.

4. Place the ball on a sheet of parchment paper and use a rolling pin to roll out to ¼-inch thick. Cut into quarters or slices.

5. Heat the cooking oil (medium heat) in a non-stick or cast-iron skillet.

6. Fry the flatbreads for about 2 minutes on each side, or until nicely browned. Turn heat down to medium, flip to cook for another minute or two.

7. Sprinkle with sea salt and keep flatbreads warm in the oven until ready to serve.

8. Top with remaining sliced avocado, sliced tomato, and microgreens.

Make-Ahead Mushroom Soufflés

Prep Time: 30 minutes

Cook Time: 15 minutes

Total Time: 45 minutes

Servings: 8

Ingredients

- 140g small button mushroom , sliced
- 50g butter , plus extra for greasing
- 25g plain flour
- 325ml milk
- 85g gruyère , finely grated, plus a little extra
- 3 large eggs , separated
- 6 teaspoon crème fraîche
- snipped chive , to serve

Instructions

1. Fry the mushrooms in the butter for about 3 mins, then remove from the heat and reserve a good spoonful. Add the flour to the rest, then

blend in the milk and return to the heat, stirring all the time to make a thick sauce. Stir in the cheese, season to taste, then leave to cool.

2. Heat oven to 400 degree F. Butter 8 x 150ml soufflé dishes and line the bases with baking paper. Stir the egg yolks into the soufflé mixture, then whisk the egg whites until stiff before folding in carefully. Spoon into the soufflé dishes and bake in a roasting tin, half-filled with cold water, for 15 mins until risen and golden. Leave to cool (they will sink, but they are meant to). You can make the soufflés up to this stage up to 2 days ahead. Cover and chill.

3. When ready to serve, turn the soufflés out of their dishes, peel off the lining paper, then put them on a baking sheet lined with small squares of baking paper. Top each soufflé with 1 tsp crème fraîche and a little cheese, then scatter with the reserved mushrooms. Bake at 375

degree F for 10-15 mins until slightly risen and warmed through. Sprinkle with chives and serve.

Grilled Goat's Cheese With Cranberry Dressing

Prep Time: 15 minutes

Cook Time: 5 minutes

Total Time: 20 minutes

Servings: 6

Ingredients

- 2 red-skinned apples
- 3 tablespoons lemon juice
- 3 x Capricorn goat's cheese , halved horizontally
- 2 tablespoons cranberry jelly
- 2 tablespoons olive oil
- 1 teaspoon clear honey
- 25g pecan

- 2 chicory heads, separated into leaves
- Handful radish sprouts (available from larger supermarkets) or watercress

Instructions

1. Quarter, core, then thinly slice the apple into a bowl with the lemon juice and 1 tbsp water. Toss well, as this stops the apples going brown.

2. Heat grill to high, then line your grill rack with foil. Put the cheeses rind-side down on the foil, then set aside for a moment.

3. Drain 2 tablespoons of the juice from the apple bowl into another small bowl and discard the rest. Add the cranberry sauce, oil and honey with some seasoning, and whisk to form a dressing. Grill the cheeses for 4 mins, then scatter the nuts on and around the cheeses and return to the grill to cook for a few mins more – but take care that the nuts don't burn.

4. Arrange the apple, chicory and radish sprouts or watercress on 6 plates, then carefully top

with the hot melted cheese. Scatter over the nuts, spoon over the dressing and serve straight away.

Spiced Carrot & Lentil Soup

Prep Time: 10 minutes

Cook Time: 15 minutes

Total Time: 25 minutes

Servings: 4

Ingredients

- 2 teaspoon cumin seeds
- pinch chilli flakes
- 2 tablespoons olive oil
- 600g carrots, washed and coarsely grated (no need to peel)
- 140g split red lentils
- 1l hot vegetable stock (from a cube is fine)

- 125ml milk (to make it dairy-free, see 'try' below)
- plain yogurt and naan bread, to serve

Instructions

1. Heat a large saucepan and dry-fry 2 teaspoon cumin seeds and a pinch of chilli flakes for 1 min, or until they start to jump around the pan and release their aromas.

2. Scoop out about half with a spoon and set aside. Add 2 tbsp olive oil, 600g coarsely grated carrots, 140g split red lentils, 1l hot vegetable stock and 125ml milk to the pan and bring to the boil.

3. Simmer for 15 mins until the lentils have swollen and softened.

4. Whizz the soup with a stick blender or in a food processor until smooth (or leave it chunky if you prefer).

5. Season to taste and finish with a dollop of plain yogurt and a sprinkling of the reserved toasted spices. Serve with warmed naan breads.

Note

USE A SOUP MAKER

Save time and effort by placing all your ingredients in a soup maker and whizzing up a delicious soup in no time.

IF YOU WANT TO USE A SLOW COOKER

Place half the cumin seeds, half the chilli flakes, the oil, carrots, lentils and 700ml stock into your slow cooker pot. Cover and cook on High for 3 hours until the lentils are tender. Dry-fry the remaining cumin seeds and chilli flakes just until fragrant. When the lentils are done, stir in the milk and whizz up the soup depending on how chunky you'd like it.

MAKE IT MOROCCAN

Substitute the chilli flakes and cumin seeds for a few teaspoons of harissa paste. You could add cooked shredded chicken at the end of cooking, too.

MAKE IT DAIRY-FREE

For a richer but dairy-free alternative, use a can of reduced-fat coconut milk instead of the milk.

Prawn & Fennel Bisque

Prep Time: 30 minutes

Cook Time: 55 minutes

Total Time: 1 hour 25 minutes

Servings: 8

Ingredients

- 450g raw tiger prawn in their shells
- 4 tablespoon olive oil
- 1 large onion , chopped
- 1 large fennel bulb , chopped, fronds reserved
- 2 carrots , chopped
- 150ml dry white wine

- 1 tablespoon brandy

- 400g can chopped tomato

- 1l fish stock

- 2 generous pinches paprika

TO SERVE

- 150ml pot double cream

- 8 tiger prawns , shelled, but tail tips left on (optional)

- Fennel fronds (optional)

Instructions

1. Shell the prawns, then fry the shells in the oil in a large pan for about 5 mins. Add the onion, fennel and carrots and cook for about 10 mins until the veg start to soften. Pour in the wine and brandy, bubble hard for about 1 min to drive off the alcohol, then add the tomatoes, stock and paprika. Cover and simmer for 30 mins. Meanwhile, chop the prawns.

2. Blitz the soup as finely as you can with a stick blender or food processor, then press through a

sieve into a bowl. Spend a bit of time really working the mixture through the sieve as this will give the soup its velvety texture.

3. Tip back into a clean pan, add the prawns and cook for 10 mins, then blitz again until smooth. You can make and chill this a day ahead or freeze it for 1 month. Thaw ovenight in the fridge. To serve, gently reheat in a pan with the cream. If garnishing, cook the 8 prawns in a little butter. Spoon into small bowls and top with the prawns and snipped fennel fronds.

Note

The prawn shells give a deep seafood flavour to this luxurious soup. It's quite a rich dish, so serve in your smallest bowls.

Mushroom & Thyme Risotto

Prep Time: 5 minutes

Cook Time: 25 minutes

Total Time: 30 minutes

Servings: 4

Ingredients

- 1 tablespoon olive oil
- 350g chestnut mushrooms , sliced
- 100g quinoa
- 1l hot vegetable stock
- 175g risotto rice
- Handful of thyme leaves
- Handful of grated parmesan or vegetarian alternative
- 50g bag rocket , to serve

Instructions

1. Heat the oil in a medium pan, sauté the mushrooms for 2-3 mins, then stir in the quinoa. Keeping the vegetable stock warm in a separate pan on a low heat, add a ladle of the stock and stir until absorbed. Stir in the rice and repeat again with the stock, until all the stock has been

used up and the rice and quinoa are tender and cooked.

2. Stir in the thyme leaves, then divide between four plates or bowls. Serve topped with grated parmesan and rocket leaves.

Red lentil, chickpea & chilli soup

Prep Time: 10 minutes

Cook Time: 25 minutes

Total Time: 35 minutes

Servings: 4

Ingredients

- 2 teaspoon cumin seeds
- large pinch chilli flakes
- 1 tablespoon olive oil
- 1 red onion, chopped
- 140g red split lentils
- 850ml vegetable stock or water

- 400g can tomatoes, whole or chopped
- 200g can chickpeas or ½ a can, drained and rinsed (freeze leftovers)
- small bunch coriander, roughly chopped (save a few leaves, to serve)
- 4 tbsp 0% Greek yogurt, to serve

Instructions

1. Heat a large saucepan and dry-fry 2 teaspoon cumin seeds and a large pinch of chilli flakes for 1 min, or until they start to jump around the pan and release their aromas.
2. Add 1 tablespoon olive oil and 1 chopped red onion, and cook for 5 mins.
3. Stir in 140g red split lentils, 850ml vegetable stock or water and a 400g can tomatoes, then bring to the boil. Simmer for 15 mins until the lentils have softened.
4. Whizz the soup with a stick blender or in a food processor until it is a rough purée, pour back

into the pan and add a 200g can drained and rinsed chickpeas.

5. Heat gently, season well and stir in a small bunch of chopped coriander, reserving a few leaves to serve. Finish with 4 tbsp 0% Greek yogurt and extra coriander leaves.

Crab & Sweetcorn Chowder

Prep Time: 5 minutes

Cook Time: 30 minutes

Total Time: 35 minutes

Servings: 4

Ingredients

- 1 onion , finely chopped
- 1 leek , green and white parts separated and sliced
- 2 carrots , chopped

- 850ml-1 litre/1.5 pints - 1.75 pints low-sodium chicken or vegetable stock
- 1 large potato , diced
- 175g/ 6oz frozen sweetcorn
- 170g can white crabmeat , drained
- 4 tablespoon light crème fraîche
- 1 teaspoon chopped chives

Instructions

1. Put the onion, white part of the leek and carrots in a large pan and pour on a few tbsp of the stock. Cook over a medium heat for about 10 mins, stirring regularly until soft. Add a splash more stock if the vegetables start to stick.

2. Add the potato, green leek and most of the stock, and simmer for 10-15 mins, until the potato is tender. Tip in the sweetcorn and crab meat, then cook for a further 1-2 mins. Remove from the heat and stir in the crème fraîche and some seasoning. Add the rest of the stock if the

soup is too thick. Sprinkle with the chives and serve with brown bread, if you like.

Chicken & Chorizo Jambalaya

Prep Time: 10 minutes

Cook Time: 45 minutes

Total Time: 55 minutes

Servings: 4

Ingredients

- 1 tablespoon olive oil
- 2 chicken breasts, chopped
- 1 onion, diced
- 1 red pepper, thinly sliced
- 2 garlic cloves, crushed
- 75g chorizo, sliced
- 1 tablespoon Cajun seasoning
- 250g long grain rice
- 400g can plum tomato

- 350ml chicken stock

Instructions

1. Heat 1 tablespoon olive oil in a large frying pan with a lid and brown 2 chopped chicken breasts for 5-8 mins until golden.
2. Remove and set aside. Tip in the 1 diced onion and cook for 3-4 mins until soft.
3. Add 1 thinly sliced red pepper, 2 crushed garlic cloves, 75g sliced chorizo and 1 tablespoon Cajun seasoning, and cook for 5 mins more.
4. Stir the chicken back in with 250g long grain rice, add the 400g can of tomatoes and 350ml chicken stock. Cover and simmer for 20-25 mins until the rice is tender.

Turkey Casserole

Prep Time: 15 minutes

Cook Time: 25 minutes

Total Time: 40 minutes

Servings: 4

Ingredients

- 2 onions, finely chopped
- 1 eating apple, cored and chopped
- 2 tablespoons olive oil
- 1 teaspoon dried sage, or 5 sage leaves, chopped
- 2 tablespoons plain flour
- 300ml vegetable or chicken stock
- 2 tablespoons wholegrain mustard
- 2 tablespoons runny honey
- 400g-500g leftover turkey, shredded
- about 350g leftover roasted vegetables like roast potatoes, parsnips, celeriacs and carrots, chunkily diced

Instructions

1. Fry the onion and apple in the oil until softened in a casserole or deep pan. Stir in the sage for 1

min, then stir in the flour. Gradually stir in the stock followed by the mustard and honey.

2. Bring up to a simmer and stir in the turkey and roast veg. Cover and gently simmer for 15 mins until turkey is piping hot. Season and eat with mash or jacket potatoes.

Apple, Pear & Cherry Compote

Prep Time: 30 minutes

Cook Time: 20 minutes

Total Time: 50 minutes

Yield: 20

Ingredients

- 8 eating apples , peeled, cored and cut into chunks
- 4 medium Bramley apples , peeled, cored and cut into chunks
- 8 firm pears , peeled, cored and thickly sliced

- 6 tablespoon sugar , or to taste
- 280g dried sour cherries (or dried cranberries)

Instructions

1. Put the apples and pears in a pan with the sugar and 50ml water. Bring to a simmer, then gently cook, covered, for 15 mins or so until the Bramley apple has collapsed to a purée and the eating apple and pear are tender (stir to make sure it doesn't catch on the bottom).

2. Stir in the cherries or cranberries for 1 min, taste and add a little more sugar if necessary. Can be chilled for 3-5 days. Serve with vanilla ice cream, if you like. See 'Goes well with' for ideas for using up the compote.

Note

IF YOU WANT TO USE A SLOW COOKER

Leave a big batch to simmer over the course of a day or night. Put the apples, pears, sugar and cherries into the slow cooker pot with 50ml of water and give it a good stir. Cover and cook on Low for 8-10 hours, until the Bramley apples have collapsed to a purée and the pears and eating apples are tender. Serve as above.

Pepper-Crusted Salmon with Garlic Chickpeas

Prep Time: 10 minutes

Cook Time: 15 minutes

Total Time: 25 minutes

Servings: 4

Ingredients

- 4 skinless salmon fillets , about 150g/5oz each
- 2 teaspoon black peppercorns
- 1 teaspoon paprika
- grated zest and juice 2 limes
- 1 tablespoon olive oil
- For the chickpeas
- 2 x 400g/14oz cans chickpeas
- 3 tablespoons olive oil

- 2 garlic cloves , finely chopped
- 150ml vegetable stock
- 130g bag baby spinach

Instructions

1. Heat oven to 375 degree F. Put the salmon fillets in a shallow ovenproof dish in a single layer. Roughly crush the peppercorns with a pestle and mortar, or tip into a cup and crush with the end of a rolling pin. Mix with the paprika, lime zest and a little sea salt. Brush the salmon lightly with oil, then sprinkle over the pepper mix. Bake for 12-15 mins until the salmon is just cooked.

2. Meanwhile, tip the chickpeas into a colander, rinse well under cold running water, then drain. Heat the oil in a pan, add the garlic, then gently cook for 5 mins without browning. Add the chickpeas and stock, then warm through.

Crush the chickpeas lightly with a potato masher, then add the spinach and stir well until the leaves are wilted. Add the lime juice and some salt and pepper, then heat through. Serve with the salmon.

Clementine, Feta & Winter Leaf Salad

Prep Time: 20 minutes

Cook Time: 0 minutes

Total Time: 20 minutes

Servings: 8

Ingredients

- 6-8 seedless clementines
- 2 heads red chicory
- 100g watercress
- 1 fennel bulb , halved, cored and very finely sliced
- 1 red onion , halved and finely sliced

- 200g feta cheese , cut into cubes
- small handful parsley , finely chopped
- For the dressing
- juice 1 clementine
- juice 1 lemon
- 4 tablespoon olive oil
- 1 teaspoon caster sugar

Instructions

1. Whisk the dressing ingredients in a jug, season with salt and set aside.

2. To make the salad, peel the clementines and slice whole. In a bowl, gently toss the chicory and watercress with the fennel and onion. Place slices of clementine on opposite sides of each plate, mound a pile of leaves in the middle, then scatter over the feta. Stir the parsley through the dressing and drizzle over the salad.

Superhealthy Salmon Burgers

Prep Time: 20 minutes

Cook Time: 10 minutes

Total Time: 30 minutes

Servings: 4

Ingredients

- 4 boneless, skinless salmon fillets, about 550g/1lb 4oz in total, cut into chunks
- 2 tablespoons Thai red curry paste
- thumb-size piece fresh root ginger, grated
- 1 teaspoon soy sauce
- 1 bunch coriander, half chopped, half leaves picked
- 1 teaspoon vegetable oil
- lemon wedges, to serve

FOR THE SALAD

- 2 carrots
- Half large or 1 small cucumber

- 2 tablespoons white wine vinegar
- 1 teaspoon golden caster sugar

Instructions

1. Tip the salmon into a food processor with the paste, ginger, soy and chopped coriander. Pulse until roughly minced. Tip out the mix and shape into 4 burgers. Heat the oil in a non-stick frying pan, then fry the burgers for 4-5 mins on each side, turning until crisp and cooked through.

2. Meanwhile, use a swivel peeler to peel strips of carrot and cucumber into a bowl. Toss with the vinegar and sugar until the sugar has dissolved, then toss through the coriander leaves. Divide the salad between 4 plates. Serve with the burgers and rice.

Note

Oily fish makes a heart-healthy alternative to red meat burgers. This recipe would also be delicious with tuna steaks.

THAI SALMON SKEWERS

Mix the curry paste, ginger, soy and oil with 1 teaspoon honey and seasoning. Marinate the salmon chunks in the curry mixture for 10 mins. Cut 1 red pepper and 1 courgette into chunks, then thread onto skewers with the salmon. Griddle for 8 mins, turning, until the salmon is cooked through.

Turkey Steaks with Citrus & Ginger Sauce

Prep Time: 40 minutes

Cook Time: 40 minutes

Total Time: 1 hour 20 minutes

Servings: 2

Ingredients

- 2 teaspoons cornflour
- 4 quick-cook turkey breast steaks, weighing about 300g/10oz total
- 1 tablespoon sunflower oil
- 3 oranges , juice of 2 and one peeled and cut into segments
- 1 teaspoon grated fresh ginger
- 1 teaspoon clear honey
- 1 pink grapefruit , peeled and cut into segments
- 1 tablespoon fresh snipped chives or chopped parsley
- wild or long grain rice and steamed broccoli, to serve

Instructions

1. Sprinkle a teaspoon cornflour onto a plate, then press the turkey steaks into the cornflour to dust them lightly. Heat the oil in a large non-stick frying pan, until it is really hot. Add the turkey and fry for 3-4 minutes, turning once

until golden on both sides – cook in batches if need be. Transfer to a plate.

2. Add the orange juice, ginger and honey to the pan. Gently bring to the boil. Mix the remaining cornflour with 1 tbsp cold water and stir into the sauce. Keep stirring on a gentle heat until thickened and syrupy, like a sweet and sour sauce. Season.

3. Return the turkey to the pan. Add the orange and grapefruit segments and heat through gently. Scatter over chives or parsley and serve straight away with rice and broccoli.

Roasties potato

Prep Time: 10 minutes

Cook Time: 1 hour

Total Time: 1 hour 10 minutes

Servings: 2

Ingredients

- 800g roasting potatoes , quartered
- 1 garlic clove , sliced
- 200ml vegetable stock (from a cube is fine)
- 2 tablespoons olive oil

Instructions

1. Heat oven to 400 degree F.
2. Put the potatoes and garlic in a roasting tin. Pour over the stock, then brush the tops of the potatoes with half the olive oil.
3. Season, then cook for 50 mins. Brush with the remaining oil and cook 10-15 mins more until the stock is absorbed and the potatoes turned brown and cooked through.

Winter Vegetable Pie

Prep Time: 15 minutes

Cook Time: 45 minutes

Total Time: 1 hour

Servings: 4

Ingredients

- 2 tablespoons olive oil
- 2 onions, sliced
- 1 tablespoon flour
- 300g (about 2 large) carrot, cut into small batons
- ½ cauliflower, broken into small florets
- 4 garlic cloves, finely sliced
- 1 rosemary sprig, leaves finely chopped
- 400g can chopped tomato
- 200g frozen pea
- 900g potato, cut into chunks
- up to 200ml/7fl oz milk

Instructions

1. Heat 1 tablespoon of the oil in a flameproof dish over a medium heat. Add the onions and cook for 10 mins until softened, then stir in the flour and cook for a further 2 mins. Add the carrots,

cauliflower, garlic and rosemary, and cook for 5 mins, stirring regularly, until they begin to soften.

2. Tip the tomatoes into the vegetables along with a can full of water. Cover with a lid and simmer for 10 mins, then remove the lid and cook for 10-15 mins more, until the sauce has thickened and the vegetables are cooked. Season, stir in the peas and cook for 1 min more.

3. Meanwhile, boil the potatoes for 10-15 mins until tender. Drain, then place back in the saucepan and mash. Stir through enough milk to reach a fairly soft consistency, then add the remaining olive oil and season.

4. Heat the grill. Spoon the hot vegetable mix into a pie dish, top with the mash and drag a fork lightly over the surface. Place under the grill for a few mins until the top is crisp golden brown.

15 Minute Low-Carb Oatmeal

Prep Time: 5 minutes

Cook Time: 10 minutes

Total Time: 15 minutes

Servings: 2

Ingredients

- 1/2 cup almond flour
- 4 tablespoons coconut flour
- 2 tablespoons flax meal
- 2 tablespoons chia seeds
- 1 teaspoon ground cinnamon
- 10 – 15 drops liquid Stevia
- 1 1/2 cup unsweetened almond milk
- 1 teaspoon vanilla extract
- Salt to taste

Instructions

1. Add the almond flour, coconut flour, flax seed powder, chia seeds, and ground cinnamon to a

mixing bowl. Whisk together until well-combined.

2. Transfer the dry ingredients to a pot over medium heat. Add the stevia drops, almond milk, and vanilla extract, then stir well.

3. Cook the oatmeal for 3 – 5 minutes until it's warmed through and starting to thicken. Remove from the heat and taste, adding salt if desired.

4. Serve the oatmeal warm with your desired low carb toppings.

Veggie Rice Pot

Prep Time: 10 minutes

Cook Time: 25 minutes

Total Time: 35 minutes

Servings: 4

Ingredients

- 1 tablespoon sunflower or groundnut oil
- 2 peppers (one red, one yellow), deseeded and thickly sliced
- 250g pack shiitake or chestnut mushrooms (I used shiitake)
- 250g long grain rice (not the easy-cook type)
- 2 garlic cloves , finely chopped
- 1 heaped tsp five-spice powder
- 3 tablespoon dry sherry (optional but worth it)
- 140g frozen petits pois
- 1 teaspoon sesame oil
- 2 eggs , beaten
- bunch spring onions , sliced diagonally
- 1 tablespoon light soy sauce , or more if you like

Instructions

1. Boil the kettle. Heat the oil in a large, deep frying pan, then add the peppers and mushrooms. Fry over a high heat for 3 mins or until starting to soften and turn golden. Turn down the heat, then stir in the rice, garlic and

five-spice. Sizzle for 2 mins, then splash in the sherry, if using, and top up with 350ml hot water.

2. Cover the pan and simmer for 15-20 mins until all of the liquid has gone and the rice is tender, stirring now and again. Add the peas for the final few mins.

3. Heat another frying pan, add a drop of the sesame oil, then add the eggs. Swirl around the pan to make a thin omelette. Once set, turn out onto a board, roll up and shred thinly. Tip the egg and spring onions onto the rice, fluff up with a fork, season with soy sauce and sesame oil, then serve.

Sweet & Sour Lentil Dhal with Grilled Aubergine

Prep Time: 10 minutes

Cook Time: 25 minutes

Total Time: 35 minutes

Servings: 2

Ingredients

- 100g red lentils , rinsed
- 1 teaspoon turmeric
- 1 tablespoon tamarind paste (we used Bart)
- 2 tablespoons vegetable oil
- 1 medium onion , thinly sliced
- 1 garlic clove , finely chopped
- 3cm/1¼ inch piece ginger , grated
- 1 teaspoon curry powder
- 1 medium aubergine , cut into 2 cm slices
- cooked basmati rice , lime or mango chutney and a few coriander leaves, to serve, if you like

Instructions

1. Cover the lentils, turmeric and tamarind paste with 500ml water. Add some salt and boil for 15 mins or until very soft. Skim off any foam that forms on the top. Meanwhile, heat 1 tbsp of the

oil and cook the onion, garlic and ginger until golden, about 5 mins.

2. Add the curry powder and cook for a further 2 mins. Pour in the lentil mixture and cook for another 10 mins.

3. Meanwhile, heat a griddle pan until very hot. Rub the remaining oil over the aubergine slices and season. Cook for 2-3 mins each side until cooked through and charred. Eat with basmati rice, lime or mango chutney and a sprinkling of coriander, if you like.

Vanilla Ice Cream

Prep Time: 10 minutes

Cook Time: 10 minutes

Total Time: 20 minutes

Yield: 8 scoops

Ingredients

- 85g golden granulated sugar or caster
- 1 ½ tsp custard powder
- 1 ½ tsp cornflour
- 500ml full-fat milk
- 2 egg yolks
- 1 vanilla pod , split in half lengthways
- 200ml carton half-fat crème fraîche
- lightly crushed raspberries or strawberries, to serve

Instructions

1. Freeze the canister from the ice-cream machine a day before you make the ice cream (if your machine requires you to). Next day, mix the sugar, custard powder and cornflour with 2 tbsp milk to make a thin paste. Beat in egg yolks. Pour the rest of the milk into a pan, scrape in the vanilla seeds, add the pod, then bring to the boil.

2. Pour this slowly over the cornflour mix, stirring all the time as you do so. Clean the pan, then

pour the milk mixture and vanilla pod back into it.

3. Cook over a medium heat, stirring all the time, until it just comes to the boil and is thick enough to coat the back of a spoon.

4. Remove from the heat, stir in the crème fraîche, then pour into a bowl. Place a piece of greaseproof paper over the surface to prevent a skin forming, then leave to cool. Put into the fridge until really cold for at least 4-5 hrs (preferably overnight).

5. Remove the paper and vanilla pod from the custard, then transfer the custard into a jug. Turn on the ice cream machine, then slowly pour in the custard.

6. Leave to churn for 10-30 mins (depending on your machine). When it stops, spoon into a plastic container, cover with cling film and a lid, then freeze for at least 3-4 hrs. (Will keep for up to 1 month. Do not re-freeze.)

7. For the best taste, remove from the freezer and soften in the fridge for 1-1½ hrs before serving. Serve with fresh fruit.

Mushroom & Tarragon Pâté

Prep Time: 15 minutes

Cook Time: 20 minutes

Total Time: 35 minutes

Servings: 4

Ingredients

- 50g unsalted butter
- 2 shallots , finely chopped
- 1 leek , finely chopped
- 2 garlic cloves , crushed
- 100g chestnut mushroom , finely chopped
- 100g shiitake mushroom , finely chopped
- 2 teaspoons wholegrain mustard
- 2 tablespoons crème fraîche

- 3 tablespoons chopped fresh tarragon , plus extra to garnish
- 1 French stick ; extra vigin olive oil; mixed salad leaves, to serve

Instructions

1. Heat butter in a large frying pan. Add shallots, leek and garlic, then gently fry for 7 mins until softened.

2. Increase the heat, add the chestnut and the shiitake mushrooms, then cook for 10 mins, stirring, until the juices have evaporated and the mushrooms are tender. Stir in the mustard and crème fraîche, then season well. Cook for a further 2 mins then stir in the chopped tarragon.

3. Preheat the grill. Cut the French stick into diagonal slices, drizzle with a little olive oil, then grill until golden. Spoon the hot pâté on to the toasts, garnish with the extra tarragon, then serve with salad leaves.

Chicken, Red Pepper & Almond Traybake

Prep Time: 15 minutes

Cook Time: 40 minutes

Total Time: 55 minutes

Servings: 4

Ingredients

- 500g boneless, skinless chicken thigh
- 3 medium red onions , cut into thick wedges
- 500g small red potato , cut into thick slices
- 2 red peppers , deseeded and cut into thick slices
- 1 garlic clove , finely chopped
- 1 teaspoon each ground cumin, smoked paprika and fennel seeds , slightly crushed
- 3 tablespoons olive oil
- zest and juice 1 lemon
- 50g whole blanched almond , roughly chopped

- 170g tub 0% Greek yogurt , to serve
- small handful parsley or coriander, chopped, to serve

Instructions

1. Heat oven to 400 degree F.
2. Place the chicken, onions, potatoes and peppers in a large bowl and season. in another bowl, mix together the garlic, spices, oil, and lemon zest and juice. Pour this over everything and spread the mixture between 2 baking trays.
3. Roast for 40 mins, turning over after 20 mins, until the chicken is cooked through. Add the almonds for the final 8 mins of cooking. Serve in bowls with a big dollop of Greek yogurt and some chopped parsley or coriander.

Juicy Lucy Pudding

Preparation and cooking time

Prep Time: 20 minutes

Cook Time: 35 minutes

Total Time: 55 minutes

Servings: 4 - 6

Ingredients

- 350g packet frozen fruits of the forest , defrosted
- 3 tablespoons light muscovado sugar
- 4 tablespoons no-added-sugar wild blueberry jam (we used St Dalfour, from larger supermarket branches)
- 6 medium-sized ripe pears , peeled, quartered and cored
- 50g fresh white breadcrumb
- 25g butter , melted

Instructions

1. Preheat the oven to 375 degree F.
2. Mix the fruits of the forest in a large bowl with the sugar and jam, then add the pears and toss to mix. Tip into a deep baking dish measuring about 18x28cm, cover with foil and roast in the

oven for 20 minutes. Pierce a pear or two to see if they are really tender; if not, return dish to the oven for another 5 minutes or until they feel soft.

3. Mix breadcrumbs with the butter and scatter over the fruit. Bake uncovered in the oven for 10-15 minutes or until golden and crispy. Serve hot.

Turkey & Parsnip Curry

Prep Time: 15 minutes

Cook Time: 35 minutes

Total Time: 50 minutes

Servings: 4

Ingredients

- 2 tablespoons vegetable oil
- 2 onions , halved through the root and thinly sliced

- 500g parsnip , peeled and cut into chunks
- 5 tablespoons Madras curry paste
- 400g can chopped tomatoes
- 500g/1lb 2oz boneless cooked turkey , cut into chunks
- 150g pot low-fat natural yogurt
- Cooked basmati rice , to serve

Instructions

1. Heat the oil in a saucepan, add the onions and fry gently for 10 minutes until they are softened and lightly coloured. Add the parsnips and stir well.

2. To make the curry, stir in the curry paste, then add the tomatoes with a little salt, and stir well. Add 1½ canfuls of water and bring to the boil. Reduce the heat, cover and simmer for 15-20 minutes, until the parsnips are just tender.

3. To finish, stir in the turkey chunks, cover the pan again and simmer for a further 5 minutes until the turkey is heated through. Remove

from the heat. (The curry can now be cooled and frozen for up to 2 months.) Lightly swirl in the yogurt and serve with basmati rice.

Note

You can add other vegetables – potatoes, carrots, celeriac or squash would all taste great. Make it go further by stirring in a drained and rinsed can of chickpeas or lentils with the turkey. Toss in a few handfuls of frozen peas or leaf spinach 3 minutes before the end.

Corn & Green Bean Cakes with Avocado & Chilli Jam

Prep Time: 10 minutes

Cook Time: 10 minutes

Total Time: 20 minutes

Servings: 4

Ingredients

- 400g sweetcorn kernels, boiled, then drained (or use 2 x 198g cans)
- 4 spring onions , chopped
- 50g green bean , chopped into 1cm pieces
- 1 red chilli (deseeded if you don't like it too hot), finely chopped
- large handful coriander leaves
- 100g self-raising flour
- 2 large eggs , beaten
- 85ml milk
- 2 small avocados , diced
- juice of 1 lime
- 2 tablespoon vegetable oil
- 250g jar Tracklemans chilli jam

Instructions

1. Put the sweetcorn, spring onions, beans, half of the chilli and coriander, the flour, eggs, milk and seasoning in a large bowl. Mix together, then set aside. Mix the avocado with the remaining chilli and coriander, the lime juice and some seasoning, then set aside.

2. Heat 1 tbsp of the oil in a large non-stick frying pan. Spoon in 6 mounds of the corn mixture, a little spaced apart. When browned on the underside, turn over and cook for a further 1-2 mins, then transfer to a plate lined with kitchen paper to keep warm. Repeat with the remaining batter.

3. Serve the cakes with the avocado salsa and chilli jam.

Cranberry Crumble Bars

These cranberry-orange bars freeze well. Make a batch on a free afternoon and pop them in the freezer so you'll always have a healthy dessert on hand when company calls.

Prep Time: 25 minutes

Cook Time: 55 minutes

Total Time: 1 hr 20 mins

Servings: 15

Ingredients

FOR THE FILLING

- 2 cups cranberries
- 1 twist Zest and juice of 1/2 orange
- 6 tablespoons granulated sugar
- 1 ½ tablespoons cornstarch
- 2 teaspoons almond extract
- ¼ teaspoon ground cinnamon

FOR THE CRUST

- 1 ½ cups all-purpose flour
- 1 ½ cups almond flour
- ½ cup granulated sugar
- 1 teaspoon baking powder

- ¼ teaspoon salt

- ¼ teaspoon ground nutmeg

- 1 twist Zest of 1/2 orange

- 4 tablespoons cold unsalted butter, cubed

- 2 eaches large egg whites

- 1 ½ teaspoons vanilla extract

- 2 teaspoons powdered sugar (Optional)

Instructions

1. Preheat oven to 375 degrees F. Line a 9x13-inch baking pan with parchment paper, letting some overhang on the long sides. (The extra will help you lift the bars out.)

2. To prepare filling: Combine cranberries, orange zest, orange juice, 6 tablespoons granulated sugar, cornstarch, almond extract, and cinnamon in a small bowl; stir well. Set aside.

3. To prepare crust: Whisk all-purpose flour, almond flour, 1/2 cup granulated sugar, baking powder, salt, nutmeg, and orange zest in a medium bowl. Work butter into the mixture,

using your hands to pinch and rub until the pieces are flattened and the mixture is crumbly and resembles sand.

4. Lightly beat egg whites and vanilla in a small bowl with a fork. Pour into the flour mixture and use the fork to scoop down from the sides and up through the center until the whites are well incorporated. Set aside 1/2 cup of the mixture.

5. Press the remaining mixture into the prepared baking pan to form a bottom crust.

6. To assemble and bake: Give the cranberry mixture a quick stir, then pour it over the crust, spreading evenly. Sprinkle the reserved crust mixture on top.

7. Bake until the top is lightly browned, about 40 minutes. Transfer to a wire rack and let the bars cool in the pan for 15 minutes. Lift the long sides of the parchment to remove and place on a cutting board. Use a sharp knife to cut into 15

bars. Cool completely. Garnish with powdered sugar before serving, if desired.

Note

If you don't have a microplane or zester, don't skip the zest. Instead, use a vegetable peeler to take just the orange part of the skin off the fruit. Leave behind as much of the white pith as possible. Then stack the strips and mince them with a sharp knife.

Sugar Substitute: Use Splenda Sugar Blend for Baking. Follow package directions to use 6 tablespoons equivalent for filling and 1/2 cup equivalent for crust. Omit powdered sugar garnish.

To make ahead: Let bars cool completely, then layer in a container or sealable bag between sheets of parchment paper. Refrigerate for up to 1 day or freeze for up to 4 months. To serve from frozen, place on a platter and let thaw for 1 hour.

Cinnamon-Raisin Oatmeal Cookies

Prep Time: 25 minutes

Cook Time: 50 minutes

Total Time: 1 hr 15 minutes

Servings: 24

Ingredients

- 1 cup white whole-wheat flour
- 1 teaspoon baking powder
- 1 teaspoon ground cinnamon
- ½ teaspoon salt
- ⅔ cup packed light brown sugar
- 6 tablespoons unsalted butter, melted
- 1 large egg
- 1 ½ teaspoons vanilla extract
- 1 cup old-fashioned rolled oats
- ½ cup raisins

Instructions

1. Preheat oven to 350 degree F. Lightly coat a baking sheet with cooking spray.

2. Whisk flour, baking powder, cinnamon and salt in a medium bowl.

3. Whisk sugar, butter, egg and vanilla in a large bowl. Add flour mixture, oats and raisins and stir with a wooden spoon until well combined. Drop level tablespoons of batter onto the prepared baking sheet, making 12 cookies per batch.

4. Bake until golden brown on the bottom, 12 to 14 minutes. Let cool on the baking sheet for 5 minutes before transferring to a wire rack to cool completely. Repeat with the remaining batter.

Sheet-Pan Chicken Fajitas

Prep Time: 20 minutes

Cook Time: 20 minutes

Total Time: 40 minutes

Servings: 4

Ingredients

- 1 pound boneless, skinless chicken breasts
- 2 tablespoons extra-virgin olive oil
- 1 tablespoon chili powder
- 2 teaspoons ground cumin
- 1 teaspoon garlic powder
- ¾ teaspoon salt
- 1 large red bell pepper, sliced
- 1 large yellow bell pepper, sliced
- 2 cups sliced red or yellow onion (about 1 large)
- 1 tablespoon lime juice
- 8 eaches corn tortillas, warmed
- Lime wedges, cilantro, sour cream, avocado and/or pico de gallo for serving

Instructions

1. Preheat oven to 400 degrees F. Coat a large rimmed baking sheet with cooking spray.

2. Cut chicken breasts in half horizontally, then slice crosswise into strips. Combine oil, chili powder, cumin, garlic powder and salt in a large bowl. Add the chicken and stir to coat with the spice mixture. Add bell peppers and onion and stir to combine. Transfer the chicken and vegetables to the prepared baking sheet and spread in an even layer.

3. Roast on the middle rack for 15 minutes. Leave the pan there and turn the broiler to high. Broil until the chicken is cooked through and the vegetables are browning in spots, about 5 minutes more. Remove from oven. Stir in lime juice.

4. Serve the chicken and vegetables in warmed tortillas accompanied by lime wedges and topped with cilantro, sour cream, avocado and/or pico de gallo, if desired.

Braised Sea Bass With Spinach

Prep Time: 50 minutes

Cook Time: 50 minutes

Total Time: 1 hour 40 minutes

Servings: 4

Ingredients

- 2 red peppers , halved, deseeded
- 2 tablespoon extra-virgin olive oil , plus extra for drizzling
- 2 shallots , chopped
- 1 garlic clove , finely chopped
- 250g cherry or baby plum tomato , halved
- small handful capers
- 12 large black olives , stoned and roughly chopped
- 20 basil leaves
- 50ml white wine
- 100ml/3½ fl oz tomato juice

- 2 whole sea bass , about 600-700g/1lb 5oz-1lb-9oz each, gutted, scaled and cleaned (get your fishmonger to do this)
- large knob butter
- 250g bag spinach

Instructions

1. Heat the grill to high. Put the peppers, skin side up, on a baking tray, then pop them under the hot grill for about 10 mins until the skins blister and blacken. Drop them into a bowl, cover with some cling film and leave until cool enough to handle. Peel away and discard the skins, then roughly chop the peppers.

2. Heat the oil over a low-ish heat in a sturdy roasting tin or in a shallow pan that has a lid and is large enough to fit both fish. Throw in the shallots and garlic and sweat briefly until soft. Stir in the tomatoes, peppers, capers, olives and half the basil leaves, then sweat for a few mins until the tomatoes soften. Pour in the wine and

tomato juice. Stir and gently simmer for 10-15 mins, adding a splash of water if the sauce becomes a bit dry.

3. While the sauce is simmering, slash each side of the fish a few times. When the sauce is ready lay the fish on top, season if you want to and cover with a lid (cover with foil if you are using a roasting tray). Leave to cook on a low heat for 12-15 mins until the flesh feels firm when pressed.

4. While the fish is cooking, melt the butter in a large pan, then fry the spinach until wilted, season if you like and divide the spinach between two serving dishes. Lift the fish carefully from the pan and place on top of the spinach, neatly drizzle some of the sauce round the fish, scatter the remaining basil on top and drizzle everything with extra-virgin olive oil. Serve with some ribbon shaped pasta, like

tagliatelle or pappardelle, with the remaining sauce in a bowl or side dish.

Baked Rotisserie Chicken

Prep Time: 10 minutes

Cook Time: 45 minutes

Total Time: 55 minutes

Servings: 8

Ingredients

- 2.5 lb chicken pieces
- 1 tablespoon Rotisserie Seasoning

Instructions

1. Preheat oven to 375 degree F.
2. Line a metal baking pan (may use disposable foil pan if desired) with foil or parchment paper and place chicken on pan.
3. Sprinkle both sides of chicken pieces with rotisserie seasoning.

4. Roast chicken 45-60 minutes or until fully cooked and thermometer registers 165 degrees F.

Notes

- Use any chicken pieces you like. Adjust the cooking time down to approx 30 minutes if using chicken wings.
- Place pieces skin side up on pan to help form crispy exterior.
- Be sure to use a pan liner for easier clean up.

Salmon Parchment Paper Boats

Prep Time: 10 minutes

Cook Time: 10 minutes

Total Time: 20 minutes

Servings: 4

Ingredients

- 40 pieces asparagus spears ends removed

- 4-6 oz thick salmon fillets skin removed
- 4 tablespoon extra virgin olive oil
- 1/4 inch ginger cut into portions and crushed
- Dash seasoning to replace salt and pepper
- 8 sprigs fresh dill plus more for garnish
- 1 piece large lemon sliced thinly

Instructions

1. Preheat your oven to 400°F and place a large rectangular piece of parchment paper on your work surface.
2. Place about 8 to 10 asparagus spears in the center but slightly off to one side of the parchment paper.
3. Place a salmon fillet over the asparagus, drizzle with a little bit of olive oil, season with Mrs. Dash seasonings (replacement to salt) and pepper then top with 3 slices of lemon and a couple of dill fronds.
4. Fold parchment paper over the salmon and seal the edges by making overlapping folds all

around the edge. At the end, tuck the final crease under the pouch to secure the seal.

5. Repeat 3 more times with remaining ingredients. Place pouches on a baking sheet.

6. Bake in the preheated oven for 10 to 12 minutes. Remove from oven, let sit for 5 minutes and then carefully cut open the parchment paper.

7. Garnish with additional fresh dill and serve immediately.

Vegetarian Tacos with Avocado

Servings: 12

Ingredients

- 1 ripe, Fresh California Avocado
- 1 ¼ cups onion, julienne strips
- 1 ½ cups sweet green pepper, julienne strips
- 1 ½ cups sweet red pepper, julienne strips
- 1 cup cilantro
- 1 1/2 cups Fresh Tomato Salsa (recipe below)

- 12 (8-inch) flour tortillas

FRESH TOMATO SALSA

- 1 cup fresh tomatoes, diced
- 1/3 cup onions, diced
- ½ clove garlic, minced
- 1/3 teaspoon jalapeño peppers, minced
- 2 teaspoon cilantro, minced
- 1 pinch cumin
- 1 1/2 teaspoon fresh lime juice

Instructions

1. Prepare fresh tomato salsa in advance. Spray skillet with non-stick cooking spray.
2. Lightly sauté the onion and green and red peppers. Mince cilantro and cut avocado into 12 slices.
3. Warm tortillas in oven or in a cast iron skillet and fill with sautéed peppers and onions, cilantro, avocado slices, and salsa.
4. Fold tortilla over and serve.

Mix together all ingredients and refrigerate.

California Avocado Brown Rice Congee

Servings: 2 - 3

Ingredients

- 5 cups vegetable stock, plus additional stock as needed
- 1 cup long-grain brown rice, rinsed and drained
- 2 tablespoons grated fresh ginger
- 4 garlic cloves, finely minced
- 1 tablespoon low sodium soy sauce (or tamari), plus additional to taste
- 1 ripe California avocado, peeled, seeded and chopped

TOPPINGS

Thinly sliced scallions, fresh cilantro leaves, toasted sesame seeds, chile garlic sauce or sriracha

Instrucctions

1. Mix the vegetable stock, brown rice, fresh ginger, and garlic together in a large pot. Bring the stock to a boil over medium-high heat, then reduce the heat to maintain a simmer

2. Simmer the congee, stirring occasionally, until the rice is cooked through and the congee has a thick, porridge consistency, approximately 90 minutes. If the congee reaches this consistency, but the rice is not fully cooked, stir in an additional 1/4 cup of vegetable stock and continue to simmer, adding additional stock as needed until the rice is fully cooked

3. When the congee is finished, remove the pot from the heat, stir in 1 tablespoon of soy sauce (or tamari), then taste. Add additional soy sauce if needed. Pour the congee into bowls and top with chunks of California avocado and any desired toppings. Serve immediately.

Shrimp, Corn and California Avocado Pasta Salad

Prep Time: 10 minutes

Cook Time: 10 minutes

Total Time: 20 minutes

Servings: 8

Ingredients

- 1 ripe Fresh California Avocado, halved, seeded and peeled
- 1 (13-oz.) box small shell whole wheat pasta, cooked and rinsed with cold water
- 1/2 lb. grilled large shrimp, shelled
- 2 grilled corn cobs, kernels cut off & cobs discarded
- 1 cup grape or cherry tomatoes, halved
- 1 cup packed fresh basil leaves
- 5 tablespoons extra-virgin olive oil
- 2 tablespoons minced shallots

- 2 tablespoons nonfat plain Greek yogurt

- 1/2 teaspoon kosher salt

- 1/2 teaspoon ground pepper

- Extra salt and pepper, to taste (optional)

Instructions

1. Cut half of the avocado into chunks and the other half into thin slices.

2. In a large bowl, combine the avocado chunks, cooked pasta, shrimp, corn kernels and tomatoes.

3. In the bowl of a food processor, combine the basil leaves, olive oil, shallots, Greek yogurt, salt and pepper. Puree until almost smooth.

4. Pour the dressing over the salad and toss gently to combine. Season with salt and pepper, to taste.

5. Lay the avocado slices on top of the pasta salad. Serve.

Healthy Green Smoothie with Chia and Peach

Prep Time: 5 minutes

Cook Time: 5 minutes

Total Time: 10 minutes

Servings: 1

Ingredients

- 1 tablespoon chia seeds
- 1 banana, ripe and ideally frozen
- 1 peach, chopped and ripe
- 1 cup unsweetened almond milk, cold
- 1 cup spinach, fresh and washed

Instructions

1. Add ingredients to blender in order listed (you want your greens on the bottom by the blade so they blend better and have the chia on the bottom to absorb some liquid before you blend).

2. Wait a couple of minutes for the chia seeds to start soaking up the almond milk.

3. Blend, and serve with your favorite toppings. Enjoy!

Note

- Spinach can be replaced with kale but the flavor will change

- You can use almost any fruit in this smoothie, it's a great way to use up leftovers.

- A frozen banana makes a big difference to the texture. It adds creaminess and thickens the smoothie almost ice-cream like and also helps keep it cool.

- I used unsweetened almond milk to avoid added sugar.

Mediterranean Fish Bake

Prep Time: 15 minutes

Cook Time: 30 minutes

Total Time: 45 minutes

Servings: 4

Ingredients

- 2 courgettes, trimmed, cut into chunks
- 2 Lebanese eggplant, trimmed, cut into chunks
- 175 gram packet petite capsicums, halved, seeded
- 1 red onion, thickly sliced
- 2 garlic cloves, sliced
- Finely grated zest and juice of 1 lemon
- 1 tablespoon olive oil
- 400 gram can diced tomatoes
- 1/4 cup Kalamata olives
- 1/4 cup parsley leaves
- 1/4 cup dill, chopped
- 4 x 150g firm white fish fillets
- 1 tablespoon pine nuts, toasted
- Couscous, lemon wedges to serve

Instruction

1. Preheat oven to moderate, 356 degree F. Spray a large baking dish with olive oil.

2. Combine courgette, eggplant, capsicum, onion, garlic and zest in the dish. Season. Pour over half the combined juice and oil.

3. Bake for 10-15 minutes until just tender.

4. Stir tomatoes, olives and half combined herbs through vegetables. Nestle fish in mixture. Drizzle with remaining oil mixture.

5. Bake for 10-15 minutes until fish flakes when tested with a skewer. Serve fish sprinkled with remaining herb mixture and nuts. Accompany with couscous and lemon wedges.

Flourless Chocolate Cupcakes with Spiced Sweet Potato Frosting

Yield: 12 cup cakes

Ingredients

- 1/2 cup millet

- 1/2 cup buckwheat groats

- 1 apple cored and cut into eights

- 1/2 cup unsweetened dried coconut

- 1/2 cup 100% pure maple syrup

- 1/2 cup cacao powder

- 3/4 cup mineral water

- 1/2 cup walnuts

- 1 teaspoon baking powder

- 1/2 teaspoon baking soda

FROSTING

- 1/2 cup cooked sweet potato

- 1/4 cups walnuts

- 3 dates pits taken out and simmered for at least 5 minutes in water

- 1/2 tablespoon 100% pure maple syrup

- 1/8 teaspoon cinnamon

Instructions

1. Soak the millet and the buckwheat overnight or for an entire day.

2. Preheat the oven to 350 degree F

3. Drain and rinse the grains and add them to the blender along with the apple, coconut, maple syrup, cacao powder, mineral water, and walnuts.

4. Blend until totally smooth, about 3 minutes.

5. Pour the batter into a mixing bowl, add the baking powder and the baking soda, and whisk just until incorporated.

6. Line your muffin tin with liners and fill each one with batter.

7. Bake for 35 minutes.

8. While the cupcakes are baking, make the frosting.

9. Place the cooked sweet potato, walnuts, dates, maple syrup, and cinnamon into the blender and blend until totally creamy and smooth, about 2 minutes.

10. Put the frosting in the fridge until the cupcakes are out of the oven and totally cool.

11. When the cupcakes are cool, spread a generous amount of frosting on each.

Pan-Fried Venison With Blackberry Sauce

Prep Time: 10 minutes

Cook Time: 15 minutes

Total Time: 25 minutes

Servings: 4

Ingredients

- 1 tablespoon olive oil
- 2 thick venison steaks, or 4 medallions
- 1 tablespoon balsamic vinegar
- 150ml beef stock (made with 2 teaspoon Knorr Touch of Taste beef concentrate)
- 2 tablespoon redcurrant jelly
- 1 garlic clove , crushed

- 85g fresh or frozen blackberry

Instructions

1. Heat the oil in a frying pan, cook the venison for 5 mins, then turn over and cook for 3-5 mins more, depending on how rare you like it and the thickness of the meat (cook for 5-6 mins on each side for well done). Lift the meat from the pan and set aside to rest.

2. Add the balsamic vinegar to the pan, then pour in the stock, redcurrant jelly and garlic. Stir over quite a high heat to blend everything together, then add the blackberries and carry on cooking until they soften. Serve with the venison, celeriac mash (see below) and broccoli.

Breakfast Cup Omelettes

Prep Time: 5 minutes

Cook Time: 12 minutes

Total Time: 17 minutes

Servings: 6

Ingredients

- 3 large eggs
- 50 ml milk
- 100 grams cheese grated
- 1 teaspoon butter
- 1 pinch salt & ground black pepper to taste
- Fillings to your preference

Instructions

1. Preheat oven to 400 degree F
2. Grease 6 holes of a muffin tin with butter
3. Whisk up the eggs & milk in a jug
4. Chop up your fillings & add some to each hole
5. Pour over the egg & milk mixture (to 3/4 full as these will rise when cooking)
6. Season to your liking
7. Top with grated cheddar

8. Cook in the oven at around for 12-15 mins or until golden

Chicken and Broccoli

Prep Time: 15 minutes

Cook Time: 35 minutes

Total Time: 50 minutes

Servings: 4

Ingredients

- 3½ lb. (1.6kg) chicken)
- 1½ lb. (70g) fresh broccoli (or 2 10 oz. (285g) packets quick-frozen broccoli)
- Boiling salted water
- 3 oz. (85g) butter
- ⅓ cup flour
- ½ cup single cream
- 2 tablespoons dry sherry
- Salt, pepper

- 2 tablespoons grated parmesan cheese
- Extra parmesan cheese

Instructions

1. Steam chicken until tender, drain, reserve 2 cups of liquid. Remove bones from chicken, cut meat into serving-sized pieces, keep hot.

2. Discard large part of stalks from fresh broccoli and most leaves. Put in boiling salted water, cook 15 minutes, drain and keep hot. (Or cook frozen broccoli according to directions on packet; drain.)

3. Melt butter in pan, stir in flour, cook 1 minute. Remove from heat, gradually add reserved liquid, blend well. Return to heat, bring to boil, stirring until sauce boils and thickens.

4. Stir in cream and sherry; season with salt and pepper. Arrange broccoli over base of ovenproof dish, pour half the sauce over. Arrange chicken pieces over sauce.

5. Add parmesan cheese to remaining sauce, pour over chicken. Sprinkle with a little extra parmesan cheese. Place under broiler (griller) or in very hot oven until sauce bubbles and is lightly browned on top.

Avocado Artichoke Pesto Stuffed Chicken

Prep Time: 20 minutes

Cook Time: 20 minutes

Total Time: 40 minutes

Servings: 4

Ingredients

- 2 ripe, Fresh California Avocados
- 1/2 cup chopped fresh basil
- ¼ cup low fat cottage cheese
- 1 tablespoon lemon juice
- 1 teaspoon crushed garlic
- 1/2 teaspoon black pepper

- 1/2 teaspoon sea salt
- 1/2 teaspoon red pepper seasoning
- 1/2 teaspoon smoked paprika
- ½ (14-oz.) can artichokes, drained and chopped
- 4 large chicken breasts
- 1 teaspoon dried basil
- 1 teaspoon thyme
- 1 teaspoon onion seasoning
- 1 teaspoon pepper flakes
- 1 teaspoon garlic powder
- 1 teaspoon sea salt

Instructions

1. In high speed blender or food processor, add all filling ingredients (avocado through smoked paprika); blend until smooth.
2. Stir in chopped artichokes. Place in fridge until needed.
3. Preheat oven to 350 degrees F. Take out chicken breast, and butterfly with knife (cut breast in

half horizontally but not all the way through so that it is still in one piece).

4. Place 1/4 filling mixture in each breast, and fold back top half of chicken to "close".

5. In a shallow bowl, mix remaining dried seasonings and salt together. Sprinkle rub mixture on each breast on both sides, and place on a cookie pan sprayed with nonstick spray.

6. Cook in oven for about 20 minutes, or until chicken is done.

Power Hour Smoothie

Prep Time: 10 minutes

Cook Time: 0 minutes

Total Time: 10 minutes

Servings: 2

Ingredients

- 1/4 ripe Fresh California Avocado, seeded, peeled and diced
- 1 tablespoon minced ginger
- 1/2 cup frozen mango cubes
- 1/3 cup plain, nonfat yogurt
- 1 tablespoon lemon juice
- Cayenne pepper, to taste
- 1 cup water
- 1 cup ice cubes

Instructions

1. Combine all ingredients in blender and puree until smooth.
2. Serve immediately.

Leafy Green Salad with Fresh Figs, Beets and Avocado

Prep Time: 15 minutes

Cook Time: 15 minutes

Total Time: 30 minutes

Servings: 6

Ingredients

- 3 cups baby spinach leaves
- 3 cups baby arugula leaves
- 1/2 cup red grape tomatoes, halved
- 1/2 cup orange grape tomatoes, halved
- 1/2 yellow bell pepper, chopped and julienned
- 1/2 cup fresh, raw beets, peeled and thinly sliced
- 1/4 cup jicama, peeled and cut into thin strips (matchsticks)
- 1 ripe, large, fresh California Avocado, seeded, peeled and diced
- 1/4 cup sliced almonds
- 1/2 cup fresh figs, quartered
- 1/4 cup feta cheese, crumbled (optional)
- 1/2 teaspoon orange zest
- 2 tablespoon almond oil

- Drizzle of balsamic glaze or aged balsamic vinegar

Instructions

1. Wash, spin dry and combine spinach and arugula leaves, and place in a large serving bowl.
2. Add red and orange tomatoes, yellow bell pepper, beets, and jicama, and gently toss with greens.
3. Top with avocado, almonds, figs, feta, and orange zest.
4. Evenly drizzle with almond oil and balsamic glaze.

California Avocado Hummus

Prep Time: 10 minutes

Cook Time: 0 minutes

Total Time: 40 minutes

Servings: 8

Prep Time: 10 minutes

Cook Time: 10 minutes

Total Time: 20 minutes

Servings: 8

Ingredients

- 2 ripe, Fresh California Avocados*, peeled and seeded
- 1 (15-oz. can) garbanzo beans (chickpeas), rinsed and drained
- 1 large cloves garlic, minced
- 1 tablespoon fresh lemon juice
- 2 tablespoon avocado or extra virgin olive oil, plus additional for garnish, optional
- 1/2 teaspoon salt, or to taste

Instructions

1. Dice half the avocado and set aside.

2. Mash remaining avocado, garbanzo beans, garlic, lemon juice, olive oil and salt together until smooth. (May also puree in blender or food processor.)
3. Gently stir diced avocado into hummus mixture.
4. Drizzle with avocado or olive oil if desired; serve.

Grapes and Grahams

Prep Time: 5 minutes

Cook Time: 0 minutes

Total Time: 5 minutes

Servings: 1

Ingredients

- 1 tablespoon light cream cheese
- 2 graham cracker squares
- ¼ cup halved grapes

Instructions

1. Spread 1 tablespoon light cream cheese on graham cracker squares and top with halved grapes.

Healing Low Sugar Protein Drink

Prep Time: 5 minutes

Cook Time: 5 minutes

Total Time: 10 minutes

Servings: 1

Ingredients

- ½ cup very cold water
- ½ cup heavy cream
- 1 cup frozen mixed berries (raspberries, strawberries, blueberries, blackberries)
- ½ tsp ground cinnamon
- ½ scoop (½ oz) vanilla protein powder

- Liquid stevia to taste (optional)
- ¼ cup ice

Instructions

1. Place all the ingredients in a blender and blend until smooth.
2. Serve immediately.

Herb-Roasted Turkey

Prep Time: 30 minutes

Cook Time: 3 hours

Total Time: 3 hours 30 minutes

Servings: 12

Ingredients

- 1 10- to 12-pound turkey
- ¼ cup fresh herbs, plus 20 whole sprigs, such as thyme, rosemary, sage, oregano and/or marjoram, divided
- 2 tablespoons canola oil
- 1 teaspoon salt

- 1 teaspoon freshly ground pepper

- Aromatics, onion, apple, lemon and/or orange, cut into 2-inch pieces (1 1/2 cups)

- 3 cups water, plus more as needed

Instructions

1. Position a rack in the lower third of the oven; preheat to 475 degrees F.

2. Remove giblets and neck from turkey cavities and reserve for making gravy. Place the turkey, breast-side up, on a rack in a large roasting pan; pat dry with paper towels. Mix minced herbs, oil, salt and pepper in a small bowl. Rub the herb mixture all over the turkey, under the skin and onto the breast meat. Place aromatics and 10 of the herb sprigs in the cavity. Tuck the wing tips under the turkey. Tie the legs together with kitchen string. Add 3 cups water and the remaining 10 herb sprigs to the pan.

3. Roast the turkey until the skin is golden brown, 45 minutes. Remove from the oven. Cover the

breast with a double layer of foil, cutting as necessary to conform to the breast.

4. Reduce oven temperature to 350° and continue roasting until an instant-read thermometer inserted into the thickest part of a thigh without touching bone registers 165°, 1 1/4 to 1 3/4 hours more. If the pan dries out, tilt the turkey to let juices run out of the cavity into the pan and add 1 cup water.

5. Transfer the turkey to a serving platter and cover with foil. (If you're making Herbed Pan Gravy, start here.) Let the turkey rest for 20 minutes. Remove string and carve.

Note

Use Large roasting pan, roasting rack, kitchen string, thermometer

Classic Beef Stew

Servings: 6

Ingredients

- 2 tablespoons all-purpose flour
- 1 pound beef stew meat, cut into 1-inch chunks
- 1 tablespoon olive oil
- 1 (8-ounce) can tomato sauce
- 3 cups water
- 1 teaspoon dried rosemary
- 1 teaspoon salt
- 1/2 teaspoon black pepper
- 2 zucchini, cut into 1/2-inch chunks
- 3 carrots, cut into 1/2-inch chunks
- 1 onion, cut into chunks
- 1 teaspoon browning and seasoning sauce

Instructions

1. Place the flour in a shallow dish; add the beef chunks, and toss to coat completely.
2. In a soup pot, heat the oil over medium-high heat. Add the beef; sauté for 8 to 10 minutes or until browned on all sides.
3. Add the tomato sauce, water, rosemary, salt, and pepper; mix well and bring to a boil.

Reduce the heat to low, cover, and simmer for 1 hour.

4. Add the remaining ingredients, increase the heat to high and return to a boil. Reduce the heat to low; simmer for 50 to 60 minutes, or until the beef and vegetables are tender, stirring occasionally.

Peanut Butter Protein Balls

Prep Time: 10 minutes

Cook Time: 10 minutes

Total Time: 20 minutes

Servings: 15

Ingredients

- 1 cup peanut butter creamy unsalted
- 1 1/4 cup vanilla protein powder
- 1/2 teaspoon vanilla extract
- 1 teaspoon cinnamon

- 2 teaspoon stevia powder
- 20 peanuts raw, unsalted

Instructions

1. Place the raw peanuts in a blender (I use my NutriBullet) and pulse several times until they become crumbly. Transfer to a plate then set aside.
2. Mix the remaining ingredients together in a bowl until smooth.
3. Roll the dough into 15 1 to 1.5 inch balls.
4. Roll the balls in the peanut crumbles and transfer them to a baking sheet lined with parchment paper.
5. Place in the refrigerator and let sit for at least 20-30 minutes.
6. Keep in the refrigerator or freeze in a sealed container up to 6 weeks.

Printed in Great Britain
by Amazon